Miracle of Max

Stephanie and
Stephen McChesney

McChesney Publishing Company LLC

The Miracle of Max
by Stephen and Stephanie McChesney

Cover concept by Madeline McChesney
Cover and Interior Layout by Karen Saunders
Edited by Jennifer Bisbing
Book production by Nobleer Media

ISBN: 979-8-9895494-0-5

Printed in the United States of America

Copies of the book may be purchased in bulk
for promotional or educational purposes.
Contact miracleofmax@gmail.com for more information.

Table of Contents

Acknowledgments

The manifestation of this book and Max's incredible story is one that is rooted in community. We want to thank our community from the bottom of our hearts for the unconditional love and support you've always given our family.

We would like to thank all of Max's doctors, teachers, coaches, and friends who have stood by his side.

We thank Karen Saunders' talented and tireless team of professionals who led us through the book production process. We appreciate Mary Walewski's expertise with social media marketing and guiding us through Amazon KDP. We also thank Jennifer Bisbing for her exceptional editing. We also acknowledge our daughter, Madeline McChesney, for the inspiring ideas for the cover concept and writing a chapter.

And above all, we want to thank our Lord and Savior, Jesus Christ. Without our faith and His hand on our lives, we would be lost.

Chapter 1 | Love at First Sight

Stephanie

"We love because he first loved us."
—1 John 4:19 (NIV)

Like most young women, I had big dreams growing up. At twenty years old, I thought I had it all planned out. My goals were illuminated with visions of opening up a skincare practice of my own and becoming a household name in the beauty industry. I imagined a life full of casting calls for my acting and modeling career, and building my business—all while building a loving family with a handsome husband. I had it all planned out in my mind.

1989

When I finished my esthetics degree, I decided it was time for me to make those dreams a reality. I was ready to start my career in helping people take care of their skin. I packed up everything I owned and moved from my hometown in Ohio to Charleston, South Carolina. It was here that I planted my roots as an esthetician. I began seeing clients, performing everything from facials to procedures, and helping people drink from the ever-sought-after fountain of youth.

New to the city and never one to not be without friends, I was determined to create a strong social circle and make my Charleston feel like home. I attended social events around town and foraged new relationships, which led me to one of the biggest blessings I would come to know.

1990

I remember the first time I set eyes on him; I was immediately filled with butterflies. His name was Stephen, and he was unlike anyone I had ever met. A friend set us up on a blind date, and as soon as we started talking, I knew he was something special. Our first date was to Josie Joe's restaurant on the water overlooking a beautiful Charleston sunset.

Once we started talking, our connection was instant—stronger than anything I've ever felt with anyone else. We understood each other from the start. I looked into his eyes and felt the connection each time we exchanged stories about growing up, our ideologies, and our goals in life. We were two dreamers who came together with the understanding that we would be stronger together than apart. We sensed we would accomplish more together than we could dream of doing alone, and that fire ignited something within us at a young age. We had the same values, the same motivated mindset, and most importantly, the desire to build a family along the way.

What could have been a short dinner date lasted for hours as we talked and talked, and I just knew. His confidence radiated through his smile, and his pure heart shined through each word.

Our months of courtship were a fairytale driven by our shared vision for the future: faith and family. It didn't take long to fall in love with Stephen once that realization settled in.

Stephen had a hope for the future, to raise a family in faith. Although our relationship was newer, he became my rock through the ebbs and flows of my work. As new challenges or conflicts would arise, Stephen stood strong for me when I needed him. Beyond that, he dreamed with me. There would be countless conversations of us enchantedly discussing our future together. He encouraged me and reminded me why I was working so hard to follow my dreams, even when I'd come home exhausted and ready to pull back.

Having someone in my corner who I could talk to about anything and everything with and who I knew would always listen and support me was incredible. We were a young couple with big hopes and dreams for the future. It was the basis of our love, and it only grew as time went on.

Time went on, and Stephen proposed. It was the easiest decision of my life—I knew our lives together would be an adventure, and I couldn't wait to take the next step.

1991

One of the first of many miracles to come in our lives was a simple piece of paper.

One day, Stephen went out to check the mail, and he stumbled upon a flyer for a local church on the ground—it wasn't even meant for us, and yet, it was. I had never really had a relationship with Christ, but we felt pulled to that church, and stepping in those doors changed our lives.

The people there were gracious, generous, and charismatic. They welcomed us, even as a young couple without children of our own. Their love of Christ shone through their words and actions. At moments when we would get distracted, they helped Stephen and I redirect our lives to center on Christ.

It was in the pews and gathering rooms that I began truly imagining life as a parent, simply because of how family oriented the church was. I had always wanted to be a mother, even since I was a little girl watching my mother show us abundant love and support throughout our lives. I wanted to be that for my children. And I was reminded of that burning desire during my time attending this church. I loved seeing all the lovely families every week, seeing all the sweet kids running around learning about the power of God. It was a beautiful thing, and it got me excited.

Shortly after we were engaged, Stephen's job took him to Atlanta. I loved the life we had created in Charleston and was sad to leave behind a city full of memories of our love story. That change was hard, as change always is. Even so, we knew good things were ahead, so we packed up our lives and headed for a new adventure in Atlanta. I began praying about it and prepared for Stephen's journey that called for this big change.

As we settled into our new life in Atlanta, we saw God working in our lives in such a profound way that we felt called to get freshwater baptized into a personal relationship with Jesus Christ. We had both been baptized into the Catholic church, but we were guided to wait so we could be freshwater baptized into a personal relationship together now. This helped us build an unbreakable foundation in our marriage and our lives.

Stepping into the water on that beautiful, sunny day was a commitment to Christ and each other. It was on that day that we chose to truly build our lives together with Christ at the center, no matter what came our way. I'm so grateful that we were baptized together before our marriage so we would always have that bond to tie us together and keep us working toward the same thing: glorifying Christ.

After a whirlwind of getting settled in Atlanta, getting baptized, and continuing to work on our future, it was finally our wedding day. The day I had always dreamed of as a little girl. I had carefully chosen every aspect of my wedding, down to the red roses and black and ivory bridesmaids' dresses. I wore my mom's wedding dress and had it restyled by a designer in Atlanta so that it was short in the front and long in the back—I had carried around a picture of that wedding dress and style in my wallet for seven years before it became a reality, and I had my total dream dress with embroidered flowers and lace applique.

I've never felt more beautiful than I did walking down the aisle of the Catholic church in Dunwoody, Georgia, with a long, cascading bouquet. I was determined to remember every moment of the special day, but it flew by in a blur. What I remember most was how full my heart felt being surrounded by family and friends. At one point, Stephen and I held on to each other and looked out across the room full of the people who mattered most to us in the world. It was a beautiful feeling.

Throughout the day, I was struck by the realization that this wasn't just one day, and it wasn't just a wedding. It was a marriage and the start of a lifelong partnership to something greater. And that's exactly what it grew to become.

During the early years of our marriage, it was a blissful blur as we learned to create a life together. Of course, it wasn't all roses. Even with our strong foundation, our marriage faced challenges early on, just as marriages do. But we were blessed with angels and miracles along the way to move us in the right direction. Each challenge brought us closer and strengthened our love even further.

1992

After just a few years of marriage, Stephen landed a new job and career in the city of his choice. We felt drawn to move to beautiful Miami. We were sad to leave our church family behind, but we felt so blessed that they had come into our lives at the perfect time.

Moving to Miami felt like the biggest step we had taken yet.

We settled into our gorgeous high-rise on the water. I had to pinch myself that this view and this life were really mine. Our hard work was paying off, and it was like fuel to our fire to keep going. We woke up in the morning and soaked in the beautiful views of the ocean before working hard to grow our businesses by day and returning home to each other at night.

Our careers were taking off. I was working as an esthetician at the Doral Saturnia Spa, now known as the Pritikin Wellness Retreat, a high-profile spa in Miami, where celebrities and dignitaries would go for their skincare services. Stephen was also growing in his profession, overseeing South Beach and Miami for Grainger.

For the first time, we lived somewhere where neither of us had family. Even so, we had each other, and we had Christ. We felt whole, all with the exception of our wish to have children of our own.

It wasn't long after our move that I found myself sitting in the bathroom waiting for the results of a pregnancy test. I was a mixed bag of every emotion—

excitement that our dreams were coming true, nervousness about providing a happy life for our child, and gratitude that we had been trusted with this beautiful gift. When that second line appeared to confirm I was pregnant, my stomach dropped. It was happening. Nothing would be the same from that moment on. It was simply indescribable.

I shared the news with Stephen, and joy overcame us both. We held each other tightly for minutes as we let the news sink in. I had dreamed of being a mother since I was a little girl, but it had always seemed like just that: a dream. Realizing that my dream was not only possible but actually happening filled me with a sense of gratitude I had never experienced before. Stephen and I had centered our lives on Christ, taken steps to follow Him, and things were working out just like we had hoped. Everything was falling into place exactly as I dreamed it, exactly as I planned it.

Realizing I was about to become a mother brought my mother to mind. I imagined what it felt like when my mother, Karen, found out that she was expecting me, and I realized the jubilation—the pure excitement, and the wee bit of nerves that came with the miracle.

My mom was the epitome of love, support, and everything I hoped to be as a mother myself. Watching her when I was a little girl and growing up with her guidance is what made me want to be a mom myself one day. I prayed I would bring her love and light with me into this new season of my life.

1994

In true Stephen fashion, he immediately dove in to make sure we did everything just right. It's one of the reasons we are such a great match—we were both determined to research, study, and learn everything about pregnancy, childbirth, and parenting. This was our new journey, and we wanted to be as prepared and knowledgeable as possible.

Stephen was all-in from the beginning. He attended all the prenatal Lamaze classes with me and was often the only male in the room. Instead of sitting back, Stephen was actively involved and constantly asked questions. But while other people were asking typical pregnancy questions about things like cravings and stretch marks, Stephen was the only one asking questions like, "If something goes wrong, what do we do?" and "What kind of blood do you use in a trauma situation?" He amazed our teacher, Karen, with his unique questions.

Becoming a parent was unfamiliar territory for both of us, and Stephen was doing everything he could to be as prepared as possible. He is a protector by nature and was thinking through every potential scenario that could happen. Christ guided him to learn and prepare to protect and help his family. We were doing everything right and hoping for the best.

I've always believed that things will go well when we do our part and keep Christ in our lives. I didn't realize that my beliefs were about to be tested.

It was early in the morning on May 27, 1994, that I jolted out of a sound sleep (or as sound as you can sleep when pregnant). As soon as I woke, I instantly knew something wasn't right. Instead of what we had learned to expect from our prenatal classes, what we saw was blood—lots of it. We quickly gathered our bags and raced to the hospital, with me sitting in the backseat with three towels to soak up all the blood.

We were scared and confused, not realizing we were about to experience the biggest trauma—and the biggest miracle—of our lives.

Chapter 2 | The Dark Room

Stephanie

> *"For you created my inmost being; you knit me together in my mother's womb. I praise you because I am fearfully and wonderfully made; your works are wonderful, I know that full well."*
>
> —*Psalm 139:13-14 (NIV)*

The drive to the hospital was a blur. My mind kept jumping through every possible scenario. We had been so prepared, and suddenly none of it mattered. Everything was going against our plan.

Was our baby safe? Would I still be able to deliver at the hospital? Would we make it through the night? I was overwhelmed by all the possible outcomes.

It was the early hours of the morning, and there were only a few cars on the road. Stars studded the sky as Stephen sped down the road. I could feel both of our energies—we were afraid. We were worried. We were questioning how exactly this could be happening, and what exactly was happening. There wasn't supposed to be any blood. Why was there so much?

"It's going to be okay, Stephanie," Stephen said in a calm and sweet voice.

Even with the calm that came through his tone, I knew we were both scared. We just wanted to get to the hospital as soon as we could.

We finally arrived. Our relief to see the ER entrance was met with a surreal moment of disbelief. The security gate was closed, and the guard was nowhere in sight.

Why is the gate closed? How could this be happening?

Our fear turned to frustration. We could see the help we needed, but we physically couldn't get through that gate. Stephen frantically honked the horn; he was ready to ram through the gate. Luckily, the security guard returned to open the gate and let us through after a few minutes.

We rushed into the waiting room. Stephen immediately demanded that someone help me. It was as if I were in a movie—dramatic hospital entrance and all. This couldn't be real life. There's no way. We had it all planned out; how did we end up here?

But when a team of nurses surrounded me in the waiting room and placed a fetal heart rate monitor on my stomach, reality sank in. Stephen realized the terror of our situation. I still didn't fully know what was happening, but I understood one thing at that moment.

God was protecting me. That brought me a sense of calm in the chaos that surrounded me. I welcomed that feeling and tried to focus on it.

Stephen, on the other hand, had a front-row seat to the traumatic scene unfolding. As the nurses rushed to check on the baby's heartbeat, Stephen watched our child flatline in the emergency room lobby. Finally understanding the gravity of the situation, the doctors whisked me back for an emergency C-section.

Stephen and I looked at each other as worry washed over us, and then he was out of sight. As soon as we arrived in the operating room, they poked my arm to hook up the IV. There was no time for a spinal tap or an epidural, so they simply put me under.

An unborn child's umbilical cord is their lifeline. That chord has three blood vessels: one that takes nutrients and oxygen from the placenta to the baby, and two that take waste back to the placenta.[1] All three vessels of the umbilical cord had ruptured, which is why blood was rushing out.

I prayed softly in my heart as I dozed off, giving everything to God.

---

[1] https://www.marchofdimes.org/find-support/topics/birth/umbilical-cord-conditions

Stephen

*"Cast all your anxiety on Him
because He cares for you."*

—*1 Peter 5:7 (NIV)*

In the moments that Stephanie was whisked away, I faced an unimaginable question: *Should I celebrate the birth of our son or prepare for the worst?*

As I sat there holding my video camera, drowning in worry and angst, I realized I had a choice to make—I could let my mind wander back to the fear that came with visualizing the worst-case scenario, or I could use that time to reflect on what God was doing in our lives.

Although it took ample effort not to slip into the fear that came with the situation, I chose to think of the latter. I took a moment, closed my eyes, and sat in stillness. I began centering myself with the hope and comfort in Jesus Christ and intentionally pulled my focus away from the dark thoughts that played in the back of my mind.

I began letting go of the situation and giving it to God. I soaked in the stillness and dug for my absolute trust in God's will. Trusting God's plan wasn't only necessary through blessings and miracles, but also during uncertainty and challenges. Sure, it became more of a challenge when something serious was on the line, but my faith could not waiver.

As I did that, I had a revelation. I suddenly heard a thought in my head that seemed like it wasn't my own. God spoke to me as I sat in that waiting room, waiting restlessly for some good news.

If your son survives, you will be the father of a special needs child.

For all our planning and questions, that was an outcome we had never considered. In that moment of shock and surprise, I felt as though the fear and angst were washed away with a newfound, God-given strength. It was as if Jesus poured courage and clarity into my cup, and I took a drink. I sat up taller, completely disbanded from fear. I stepped confidently into faith, knowing that with God by our side, we could face any outcome.

Buoyed by that revelation, I looked up to see Karen, our Lamaze teacher. Of all the people we knew in Miami, she was one of the last people he expected to see. We hadn't even had time to call and tell her Stephanie was in labor. It was divine timing. Karen had come in for her shift, and I was relieved to see her. Since I couldn't go back to the operating room, I asked Karen if she could do it instead.

"Karen, it's nice to see you. Stephanie is having the baby right now, they took her back a little bit ago. Would you mind going in to check on her?"

"Sure, Stephen, no problem!" she said, cheerfully.

She had no idea what had transpired in the last few hours. The last she knew, Stephanie had a perfectly healthy and unproblematic pregnancy. And so, she went to check on Stephanie, excited to be there for a new arrival.

Two minutes passed, and Karen returned. She was white as a ghost and couldn't even talk to me, nor did she look at me. She ran past the waiting room and down the hallway to the surgery door. This interaction obviously did nothing to calm my nerves, and the game of tug-of-war between faith and fear commenced once more.

But back behind those hospital doors, miracles were taking place.

Chapter 3 | Keep Going

Dr. Tony

> *"Jesus looked at them and said,*
> *'With man this is impossible,*
> *but with God all things are possible.'"*
>
> *—Matthew 19:26 (NIV)*

It was another day. I dragged myself out of bed, got ready, and headed to the hospital to begin my shift. It felt like any other day—I felt tired. Unmotivated. I felt anxious most mornings as I made my drive to the hospital. I wasn't happy. I had lost my luster for my work, and it felt like I was just going through the motions.

I had been doing this for years, and I'd been so consumed in the routine that I didn't pay much attention elsewhere. My personal life had been compromised, and I worked so much that my relationships floundered. On this particular morning, I felt like I was done.

Maybe it was time for me to do something else. This career had become mundane and unfulfilling. Most days I questioned everything I was doing, although it was particularly strong this morning. Even so, I continued to go through the motions.

The clock ticked through my day. It was the usual—I helped patients, checked in on others, had a snack—the broken record player. But one thing I did, that wasn't on the typical to-do list, was to check on the blood supply.

As my night shift was coming to an end, I saw my colleagues frantically running to the labor and delivery unit. Within seconds, I heard on the intercom that there was a code blue in the labor and delivery operating room.

Something came over me. I raced across the hospital and got there just as the baby was delivered. He was white as a sheet of paper. I had never seen such a ghostly white child in my thirty years of practicing medicine.

Within minutes of childbirth, the doctors and nurses give babies an Apgar score in five key areas: color, heart rate, reflexes, muscle tone, and respiration. The score is on a scale of zero to two. Most babies earn twos, with the occasional one after a traumatic pregnancy or delivery. This baby had an Apgar score of zeros in every area—he was in critical condition.

I realized we had no time to waste. First, I began giving the baby a blood transfusion, and then I began performing infant CPR on this tiny, pale body.

The room went quiet, filled only by the sound of my gentle yet firm thumps on the baby's chest. While I performed CPR, it seemed as though everyone else in the room was praying.

Five minutes passed—nothing. But, I continued.

Ten minutes passed. The ticking of the clock began to overtake the thumps on this baby boy's chest. It felt like an eternity, but there was something else driving me. I felt relentless. I continued without a glimmer of hope in sight.

Fifteen minutes passed—still nothing. With CPR, you have to be incredibly consistent if you want it to work. And by God, I wanted it to work. It felt bigger than me.

Something told me to keep going. A voice in my head kept telling me not to stop on this child.

Don't stop until he wakes up.

Eighteen minutes.

Nineteen minutes.

Twenty minutes.

The baby kicked.

After twenty harrowing minutes of tireless effort, it happened! The boy's heartbeat came back, followed by his faint breath.

He was alive.

The other doctors and nurses took over from that moment to get the baby to the Neonatal Intensive Care Unit, and I looked at the mother, who was asleep on the operating bed. The doctors had finished the cesarean, and she lay there still as her body recovered. A sense of calm overtook the room, and I sat there looking at this miracle.

The baby was gone for twenty minutes—no heartbeat, nothing. And yet, here he was. His little body was beginning to breathe and move. He was back.

It was a miracle.

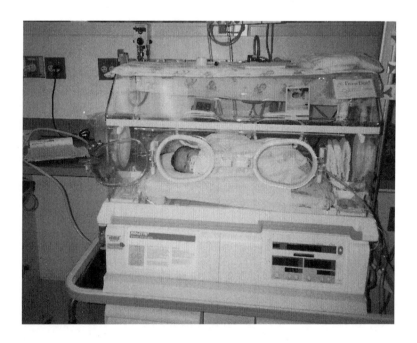

Chapter 4 | God's Grace

Stephanie

"But He said to me, 'My grace is sufficient
for you, for my power is made perfect in
weakness.' Therefore I will boast all the more
gladly about my weaknesses, so that Christ's
power may rest on me. That is why, for Christ's
sake, I delight in weaknesses, in insults, in
hardships, in persecutions, in difficulties.
For when I am weak, then I am strong."
—2 Corinthians 12:9-10 (NIV)

Seeing Max for the first time wasn't how I had imagined meeting my baby. Instead of sweet newborn cuddles in the afterglow of labor and delivery, it became a moment of rebound. The attention had been on Max, but my body had also gone through a traumatic event. The doctors and nurses wouldn't let me move and wanted to make sure I was stable before I could see Max.

I didn't care; I just wanted to see my son. Nine months of waiting! I wanted to see him—to see what he would look like, how big he was, and who he resembled. It was a year of wonder, and when the moment actually came, it was something we never would have imagined would happen.

The nurses wheeled me into the NICU, where Max was sleeping. His sweet little body was covered in wires. He was so tiny and needed the help of large machines to stay alive. It broke my heart. He was so covered in wires that it was difficult to see his face. But what I did see was beautiful.

He was my perfect baby boy.

My heart broke as I gazed at him. My eyes welled with tears, and my stomach sank thinking about how I wished I could just take his pain away and heal him. As I tried to make sense of all the emotions of that moment, I saw God's face and heard His voice—

He's going to be okay.

A rush of stillness came over me, and I felt as though I was being held up by Him. I held on to that sense of calm, and it brought me an unwavering faith I had never felt before. As the days went on, I would remind myself of this moment. I would think back and feel God's reassurance come over me. It brought me comfort as we adjusted to the uncertainty.

We heard a knock on the door. It was one of the doctors. He introduced himself as Dr. Tony, the anesthesiologist who had resuscitated Max, and he started balling.

He kept looking at Max, then looking at me. He was incredibly emotional, working to catch his breath as he spoke with us. And then he opened up and told us about having a hard time deciding whether he was going to stay in his profession.

"This whole trial has changed my life forever," he said.

I was taken aback and tears came to my eyes as we thanked him for sharing.

That moment touched both Stephen's and my heart.

Regardless, I knew this was the beginning of a long and difficult road. The motherhood journey I had dreamed about had changed in an instant. It went from excitement to angst because of the uncertainty we faced. But receiving that strong comfort from God was a turning point that gave me inner strength. Even with my world turned upside down and my body aching, I knew this would be a positive experience.

For two weeks, Max slept in the NICU with the wires and machines as his constant companions. We visited whenever possible, and my deepest need and request was to hold Max. But I couldn't yet. Those two weeks seemed to drag on forever as I waited to hold the baby I had dreamed of for so long.

The problem was that Max's kidneys weren't working, and the hospital staff worried that moving or unplugging him from the machines would cause further issues. So, we waited for a miracle.

During those first few days, Max received more treatments than most adults receive in their entire lifetime, including a blood transfusion and kidney medications. It seemed like every day brought another setback or unexpected procedure. It was draining emotionally, but it could have been so much worse, and knowing Max was alive kept us going.

I held on to that comfort I had received when I first saw Max. Despite all the challenges, we were hopeful for the future and ready to walk the road. We prayed for Max's wellness; we prayed for strength; we prayed for all his caregivers.

We stood strong in our faith, and through that, we learned that there is magic in faith. It was as if we built a wall around our minds, and fear and anxiety banged on the doors trying to get in. And when that fear and anxiety started to creep in, we would turn our attention back to God. We would pray more, and we would pray harder. Not just a prayer with words, but a prayer with feeling, believing, and receiving. These were prayers that came from the depths of our hearts. There were also many people all over the world praying for us!

With that level of faith, we were able to stay positive. We could see the light through the darkness and feel stillness in the discord.

Don't get me wrong, it was a challenge. We were the center of a whirlwind of medical opinions, ideas, and recommendations. We had positive and negative people around us, and we were expected to trust and listen to all of them. But we had something bigger than that guiding us through the uncertainty.

As the days went on, it was important to me that we surround Max with positivity. We didn't need any negativity near him. We didn't need it around us, for that matter. Neither Stephen nor I could stomach doubt, and we wanted to dismiss the "realists" who gave us the hard facts about Max. We were hoping for a miracle. This was bigger than us. We knew in our hearts and our faith that all things are possible through Christ.

We needed to be around those who believed in miracles. I even told all of my family and friends to not be negative around me or ask anything foolish. Only positive energy and encouragement would be around me and my family as we worked through this. Even so, we talked to doctors who were pessimistic about Max's condition every day. It was draining.

They belittled us for believing that Max would recover and thrive, but by the power of the Holy Spirit, we pushed through the negativity. Through it all, we had one doctor who we loved and appreciated: Dr. Bloom, our NICU doctor. He recognized that the chances were slim, but he knew there was a chance. While all the other doctors held on tight to the 80 percent chance that Max wouldn't make it, Dr. Bloom believed that Max would fall into the 20 percent who survived.

We had already experienced a miracle, and we knew what was possible.

There was another angel looking over Max through his days in the NICU. Lisa Fowler was a neonatal nurse and watched over Max. She provided physical care for him and took care of him every day. Beyond her regular duties, she also provided spiritual care for Max.

She would let no one speak negatively about him or his situation. Lisa brought positive words to anyone who spoke negatively about Max. She came into our room one early morning and said, "I want you to know I am watching and praying over Max daily. I am overseeing what is going on in this room, and it *will* be positive." Her support made all the difference in a sea of negativity.

As the days went on, we received a call from Stephen's boss, Jim Marraro. Jim was calling to check in and see how everything was going. He was a charismatic Christian man who had mentored and supported Stephen. His call was right in line with his attitude of service.

For more than thirty minutes, Jim prayed for Max with me over the phone, offering incredible comfort as he pleaded with God for a miracle. It was the first time we had seen anyone stop and pray with someone, and it brought more strength than I could have imagined. We knew we had God on our side, but listening to those prayers helped me realize we were also building our community. We had people who truly cared and wanted to help.

We were young and alone, with just our church community and neighbors. We had to dig deep for strength, and as we turned to God, a powerful strength would come over us.

I never knew I had it in me to get through this situation, but that strength appeared just when I needed it. There were a lot of tough times, but they were matched with ample wisdom and strength.

Through this, we grew. We grew as people; we grew as believers; we grew as a family.

Chapter 5 | Whose Plan?

Stephen

> *"Do not be anxious about anything, but in every situation, by prayer and petition, with thanksgiving, present your requests to God. And the peace of God, which transcends all understanding, will guard your hearts and your minds in Christ Jesus."*
>
> —*Philippians 4:6-7 (NIV)*

The gravity of the situation sank deeper with each new day at the hospital. There was little change in Max's condition, and we still weren't able to hold our baby boy.

Despite our positivity and the angels around us, things didn't seem to be getting better. After nearly three weeks in the hospital, Max's body was growing toxic. His tiny kidneys were shutting down and poisoning themselves. Things were grim, and every day felt like a parade of bad news. Max couldn't urinate, and his body was holding on to all the toxins. We were being told we might need to talk to a nephrologist about dialysis.

We tried to stay optimistic, but the weight of Max's condition and our outlook for the future wore us down every day. In our hearts, we knew those feelings of doubt and fear weren't from God. But some days, I couldn't shake feelings of dread and worry. Surely, there had to be another miracle. There had to be.

As the situation in the hospital grew more dire, I turned again to my boss, Jim Marraro, for daily uplift. On one tough day when Max was just a few weeks old, I explained the severity of Max's condition and asked what I should do. I remember him clearly telling me that if he were me, he would attend a healing service at his church in Fort Lauderdale, where there was a famous healer passing through and holding a service that night. I was quizzical—did I need to drive an hour for the off chance of healing our boy? My time could be better spent watching over my wife and son at the hospital. Even so, I knew we didn't have many other options. Stewing around the hospital was emotionally draining and futile. So, I kissed Stephanie goodbye and hopped in the car to drive north.

I arrived at a large church and walked through the doors feeling drained and skeptical with little energy to give, but I was hopeful for a miracle. I sat down in the back row and watched the service with hesitation, trying to keep my mind in the room rather than elsewhere with Stephanie and Max.

The healer stated, God gives all kinds of spiritual gifts to individuals, but for some reason, he was blessed with the ability to heal in Jesus's name. He seemed humble and shared stories of holding services in foreign lands, leading people to Christ, and healing many. He then invited people to come up and get prayed over.

One by one, people walked up to the stage. As they did, the healer placed his hand on their shoulder and began to pray. Some people sat there in silence, others began to weep. Music played in the background and miracles seemed to be happening before my eyes. Even so, I stayed skeptical and firm in my seat.

I felt defeated. After weeks in the hospital and having near-death experiences, I didn't see how someone I didn't know would save my child. Max was miles away in the hospital—how could he possibly be healed that night?

I was getting ready to leave, convinced the trip had been a waste of time, when I heard words from the stage that pierced my heart. "I feel like there is someone who hasn't come up, and it has to do with kidney failure," said the healer.

The hair on the back of my neck stood up. I knew he was talking to me, and I knew it was about our tiny baby. Instantly, my skepticism was erased. I knew this was God's message to me. The spirit of God led me to the front of the room, where I shook the healer's hand. I was moved to tears as I told the story of Max, his kidney situation, and all we had been through.

Calmly and lovingly, the healer took my hands, looked me in the eyes, and said, "Your son is going to be fine." Then he handed me a vial of oil and a handkerchief. He gave me instructions on how to anoint Max with the oil in the name of the Father, the Son, and the Holy Spirit.

My heart was changed. I left the room the opposite way I had arrived—renewed and rejuvenated with positivity and faith. I was hopeful, and I couldn't wait to get back to Stephanie and Max.

It was about eleven p.m. when I got back to the hospital. Stephanie was waiting, anxious to hear about the healing service. I wasted no time telling her about the healer's instructions and the spirit of God that had overcome me at that moment.

I was hopeful. I was confident in my faith. I was excited for the possibility of another miracle.

This was the answer we had prayed for. Stephanie begged me not to wait any longer.

We quickly followed the pastor's instructions, anointing the oil and placing it on the handkerchief over Max. Minutes passed until the nurse came to check Max's diaper, just as she had done multiple times every day for weeks. And every time, the diaper had been dry, a sign that Max's kidneys continued to shut down. But this time, just moments after we anointed Max with oil, things were different.

The nurse stood there in shock, unable to believe her eyes. Instead of a quick check on a dry diaper, she had to use both hands to hold Max's diaper because it was so full. His kidneys were working.

It was a miracle.

The next morning, the entire hospital was buzzing about the miracle of Max. The doctors and nurses filled our room and expressed their amazement. They couldn't believe his incredible turnaround. We were ecstatic that our baby boy was on the up and up, and we recognized how much God's love played a role in this experience.

Many doctors and nurses questioned whether Max would make it. But, we knew the miracle had come from our loving God.

Sometimes, the only thing you can do is pray. The only thing you can have is faith. When all else seems to be falling apart, your belief and hope that everything is in God's hands is what will change the dynamic.

In situations where life feels out of control and everything seems to be crumbling beneath your feet, it's difficult not to let fear into your heart. It's easy to spiral into worry and angst. The unknown can be terrifying, especially when it's something that is near and dear to you. Far too often, we as human beings, fall into a victim mentality. We ask, "Why is this happening to me?" That's exactly what the devil wants you to do.

He wants you to worry. He wants you to feel fear, question yourself, question the situations at hand, and question God. You have to draw a line in the sand. Build the wall in your mind. Seek out the light, no matter how dark the room may get. It's up to us. After all, God granted each of us free will.

Don't allow negative thoughts into your mind or negative words onto your lips that speak anything other than faith and hope. When the fear overtakes you, stop the train of thought and simply pray. Turn to God and seek His guidance, strength, and peace.

Even when everything goes haywire, and it feels like nothing is going how you thought it would, you can't spiral into fear or negativity. Hold your faith. Through prayer, positive thinking, and awareness, God can change any situation.

We go through life with a plan in mind—a birth plan, a career plan, a dream, a wish. We can do everything in our power to stick to the plan, but it may differ from what God has in store for us. And when things don't go according to our own plans, it can feel like the world is ending. It feels like everything we hoped for and dreamed of is being taken away from us. It hurts, and it's a struggle.

We wonder what God's plan could possibly be when everything is going so "wrong." We wonder how this will be connected to the future. But God knows what He's doing. He designs our lives in a way that everything is either a blessing or a blessing in disguise. And so long as we trust His will and stay positive, miracles can occur.

And they did.

The best part? This was only the beginning of the *miracle* of Max!

Chapter 6 | Home Sweet Home

Stephanie

"Do not conform to the pattern of this world, but be transformed by the renewing of your mind."

—Romans 12:2 (NIV)

"And we know that in all things God works for the good of those who love him, who [I] have been called according to his purpose."

—Romans 8:28 (NIV)

After weeks at the hospital, we were finally discharged to take our sweet baby boy home. The full days and nights that followed, Stephen and I were on constant alert. We got little sleep and checked often that Max was still breathing, just as every first-time parent does. With Max, the risks were a bit higher.

A couple of days later, Max had his first regular doctor's appointment. We went to see Dr. Froinleck, Max's nephrologist. His vitals were good, but when the doctor went to do a blood count on Max's kidneys, he discovered Max's BUN was way up, a sign that things weren't working properly.

"We need to take care of this," said Dr. Froinleck. "Meet me at Joe DiMaggio Hospital."

I was a nervous wreck. Just when I thought we had dodged a bullet, we were back in the big risks again. Max was checked into yet another hospital. This time, however, he was under the care of the top kidney doctor in Miami. Dr. Froinleck took good care of Max and put him on medications to see how we could get his kidneys stable independently.

Through all of this, Stephen was trying to hold on to his job, and I was trying to help Max. Our families that lived out of state didn't understand exactly what we were going through; they weren't there to see it. Our friends had a hard time understanding it as well. We slowly began growing apart from the people we thought would be holding our hands through it all. It felt very lonely.

Days passed as Max rested and recovered at the new hospital. I remember walking around Joe DiMaggio's statue, and with each step, my heart would break. There were a lot of children dying in those hospital rooms—cancer, illness, different ailments—it was heartbreaking. I prayed for each of those children as I went from room to room, and at that moment, I realized, by the grace of God, I needed to stand tall and become a warrior mom. It was a pivotal moment that I would realize later changed the course of our lives.

We needed to be in a positive environment. I came back and told the doctor that it was time for us to get out of there. Being in a hospital, with that level of troubling worry surrounding us, wasn't helping us. It was only hurting us. I pleaded with Dr. Freundlich to let us go home. I persuaded him of my ability to facilitate all the medications, and he agreed. He and his team walked me through everything I needed to do to properly care for my boy and get his kidneys working. Once I felt confident and had what we needed, they let us go.

We were home once more.

The dreams I once had of newborn snuggles and cuddling naps were replaced by a full schedule of doctors and therapist appointments. At just one month old, Max had a team of eight doctors, each treating a different condition. With so many doctors and appointments, it becomes hard to discern how to eliminate appointments and doctors that are not necessary.

Beyond just doctors, there are other people consistently directing you on what to do. Even so, when *you* are a parent, *you* have the intuition that guides you. If you have a strong relationship with God, you will get direction. You must trust that. Sure, consider and do your due diligence, but don't allow your fear to keep you from advocating for your child.

But as we narrowed down the symptoms and ran tests, we slowly saw fewer and fewer doctors. We were getting closer to a diagnosis.

I tried to stay strong as a young first-time mom, but it was hard with no family around. Stephen was an incredible support, but he was also trying to hang on to his job. He felt pulled in multiple directions and spread thin. He wanted to be there to support his new family of three, but he also needed a job to be able to support us. It was a no-win situation.

It would have been easy to wallow and focus on the negative. We faced roadblocks, bad news, and poor test results every day—not to mention the usual challenges of learning how to take care of a newborn baby for the first time.

But during those dark days, I felt God's strength like never before. I knew I had to be tough and move forward if I wanted to see my son and my family succeed.

One day, I was sitting at home with Max, just the two of us. I marveled at his tiny fingers and button nose when I was struck with an incredible feeling that Max would overcome all the obstacles and someday tell his story. Small experiences like that of God's support and love became regular occurrences. They gave me the strength to be strong for Max and Stephen because I knew God was on our side.

I knew without a doubt that Max would overcome his obstacles. But that didn't mean the people around us believed. We were often surrounded by negativity.

and bad news. It would have been easy to give in and listen to all the pessimism. But I knew that how I responded to the situation would be how people acted around Max.

If I was negative and didn't have hope for the future, others would follow suit. If I acted like I didn't believe he could do something, others would agree. But if I stood up for Max and shared my conviction that he would overcome his challenges with the strength of the Lord, people around me would listen and agree. It's amazing how positivity spreads. I saw incredible changes in people's dispositions and attitudes toward Max when I shared my beliefs in him.

But, as anyone who has been the rock in a difficult situation, staying positive and strong can be draining. Emotionally, we were starting to break apart. As difficult as things were, we never gave in to the victim mentality. There were times of frustration, feeling overwhelmed, and meetings and news that brought us to our knees. But we never had a woe-is-me moment.

During those frustrating times, we remembered God's grace and the vision I had when I first saw Max. I remembered those words from the Lord—

He's going to be okay.

In times of prolonged stress, whether it's a situation like ours, a divorce, losing a job, or thousands of other things that go wrong in life, it's common for people to fall into a victim mentality. Through times of hardship and discomfort, you are in spiritual warfare. But we need to be aware of the attributes of the victim mentality to catch ourselves before we spiral too far. When we slip into a victim mentality, we look for things to go wrong and blame others. We don't think we have the power to change our mindset or our situation.[2]

Succumbing to a victim mentality seems easier.

When you understand Satan's traps to pull you into a victim mentality, you can (and must) protect yourself with God's armor. Just because something bad happens doesn't mean life is bad. When you're in tune with God, staying in the light and finding the meaning behind the challenge is possible. That meaning can very well be your life's purpose.

The Lord had my back. That knowledge gave me daily encouragement as I worked with God to combat the victim mentality. That attitude required daily effort, but I know that what we put in is what we get out. I was putting in faith and positivity to make the most of a difficult situation.

After months of constant doctor's appointments and tests, we sat in the doctor's office on a sunny Miami day when Max was eight months old to receive his diagnosis: he had minor cerebral palsy. It didn't come as a surprise to us because Max's head circumference

---

2   Rocco Marinelli, "The Prevalence of a Victim Mentality in Today's Society," (Medium, 2020). Accessed on 12/6/23, https://medium.com/@roccomarinelli/the-prevalence-of-a-victim-mentality-in-todays-society-7e516821cf75

hadn't grown since the last appointment, and the nurses had told us it was a possibility. On the one hand, the news brought closure; on the other hand, it opened up new questions and possibilities.

We were referred to a pediatric neurologist at Miami Children's named Dr. Sara, who told us that Max's journey would differ from what we probably had expected. Even so, he would succeed.

The doctor looked into my eyes and said, "I know this child will do well. He has you as a mom, and you are like no one I've ever met. You are a fighter!"

As we walked out of the hospital that day, Stephen noticed a beautiful poem in the lobby. The words echoed our situation and lifted my soul after a challenging few months.

Welcome to Holland

Written by Emily Perl Kingsley

I am often asked to describe the experience of raising a child with a disability—to try to help people who have not shared that unique experience to understand it, to imagine how it would feel. It's like this . . .

When you're going to have a baby, it's like planning a fabulous vacation trip—

to Italy. You buy a bunch of guidebooks and make your wonderful plans. The Coliseum, the Michelangelo David, the gondolas in Venice. You may learn some handy phrases in Italian. It's all very exciting.

After months of eager anticipation, the day finally arrives. You pack your bags and off you go. Several hours later, the plane lands. The stewardess comes in and says, "Welcome to Holland."

"Holland?!" you say. "What do you mean, Holland?" I signed up for Italy! I'm supposed to be in Italy. All my life I've dreamed of going to Italy.

But there's been a change in the flight plan. They've landed in Holland and there you must stay.

The important thing is that they haven't taken you to some horrible, disgusting, filthy place, full of pestilence, famine and disease. It's just a different place.

So you must go out and buy a new guidebook. And you must learn a whole new language. And you will meet a

41

*whole new group of people you would
never have met.*

*It's just a different place. It's slower paced
than Italy, less flashy than Italy. But
after you've been there for a while and
you catch your breath, you look around,
and you begin to notice that Holland has
windmills, Holland has tulips, Holland
even has Rembrandts.*

*But everyone you know is busy coming
and going from Italy, and they're all
bragging about what a wonderful time
they had there. And for the rest of your
life you will say, "Yes, that's where I
was supposed to go. That's what I had
planned."*

*The pain of that will never, ever, go away,
because the loss of that dream is a very
significant loss.*

*But if you spend your life mourning the
fact that you didn't get to Italy, you may
never be free to enjoy the very special, the
very lovely things about Holland.*

But that was just the beginning. As I walked Max
to the car and strapped him into the car seat, I felt

surrounded by God's presence. It was like He was right there with me and I could reach out and touch and hug him.

That's when God told me,

I get it.

It was life-changing to realize how personally God understood me and my situation. He knew exactly what we were going through and was there to support us, always.

I sat in the parking lot praying and giving glory to God with tears in my eyes. That day changed my life forever. It wasn't the diagnosis that changed us; it was knowing my mission and what God had called Stephen and me to do.

Years after Max's traumatic birth in Miami, where he was brought back to life, we returned to the hospital for an anniversary honoring kids who had been in intensive care. We had barely stepped in the door when Dr. Bloom, the NICU doctor, started to tear up. Stephen noticed it.

"What are you thinking about, Dr. Bloom?" Stephen asked, kindly.

With tears in his eyes, he told us that kids who go through trauma always have delayed dental work, sometimes lasting their entire lives. Dr. Bloom had seen Max's smile and full set of healthy teeth and was amazed.

It was another miracle—one I didn't expect. I never thought Max wouldn't have those teeth. I always knew that Max would recover and live the full and beautiful life he has. Teeth may seem small in the grand scheme of things, but they show how God cares about every detail of our lives.

Max's story wasn't a mishap or a mistake. It didn't turn us into victims. It turned us into victors! It was fate, and it turned us into true believers to glorify God in all that we did going forward.

Chapter 7 | Our Sweet Toddler

Stephanie

> *"I can do all this through Christ*
> *who gives me strength."*
> —*Philippians 4:13 (NIV)*

Max grew. He grew from our sweet little baby to our joyous toddler, and each day came with more and more love. When people ask me what Max was like as a child, the answer is simple: A total joy of the Lord!

For all the difficulties we faced in Max's first few weeks and months, the toddler years counteracted it. The days were full of mac and cheese and building blocks, just like any other toddler. He loved to play, and we loved to play with him. Being his parents and watching him learn and grow brought us a sense of fulfillment we had not yet known. And his sweet, positive, and light-hearted attitude shined even at that young of an age. No matter the situation, Max's positive attitude was infectious.

As a toddler, Max was a happy boy. He was a fighter from the beginning, resilient as could be, all while bringing the bubbly side of his personality into the mix to lighten things up. He made people laugh and smile, being his playful self. Max had the most infectious laugh that couldn't help but make you smile.

In those early days, it would have been easy to imagine all the challenges and difficulties ahead. As a parent, I was already thinking years ahead—school, friends, everything . . . There were questions that ran through my mind as I watched him tumble a ball across the yard. Which school would be the most inclusive, what programs are available for him as he gets older? What will happen as he starts making friends? Will people be nice to him? Will he be okay?

But it was in those moments that God showed up big and showered me with His grace. I trusted Him, and in return, He brought me comfort and understanding. We could see Max shine the light of the Lord, and any question in my mind was matched with a vision of Max bringing unimaginable joy into our lives and the lives of others around us.

It was at this time we realized we didn't want to raise our family in Miami. My parents had retired to Murrells Inlet, South Carolina, and we felt it would be beneficial to be near them. God opened a door for us in Anderson, South Carolina. We moved there on a prayer—sight unseen.

We wanted to enable Max to fulfill what he was put here to do. In order to do that, we had to be intentional in how we raised him.

The one thing that hinders a family with a child with special needs is parents who baby the child and *act* like they have special needs. That was not going to be the case with my son. There was nothing different about him. In my mind, we all have special needs; we are all different in some way or another. Stephen and I decided early on not to put limits on Max. We wanted him to try *anything* and *everything*. We wanted him to experience the world, and find what made him happy.

No limits.

He was like any other child, and we were going to treat him as such. As his parents, we wanted to offer him every chance to be successful in any way we could. God's grace had supported Max from day one. Max knew he wasn't different from anyone else. He could do anything and everything through Christ. So even early on, we introduced new things to him on a regular basis, whether it was new foods or new activities. Even so, just because we encouraged Max to try something doesn't mean it always came easy to him. It took the extra effort, time, and encouragement to get him to achieve different things. Take, for instance, playing catch.

Each day, Stephen and I spent time throwing the ball back and forth with Max. It took Max longer to learn to throw and catch a baseball, but every time the ball came toward him, he tried to catch it with the same excitement and tenacity as the time before. His light never flickered, it never dwindled. He stayed committed and positive.

The day came when he caught the ball on his own, and as his face broke into an incredible smile, we couldn't help but beam. We were so proud of him every step of the way, and more importantly, he was proud of himself.

We knew Max didn't need special treatment. He was capable; he was able. Disability or not, he had a fire within him and a God-given purpose. I knew this deep down, and I wanted others to know it too. That desire led to me becoming overprotective.

He was my boy.

It was hard not to jump in and help him when things were hard or give him a boost when he was stuck. I wanted to be there for him at the drop of a hat, but I also realized that I couldn't do that. With wisdom from the Lord, I realized I shouldn't *always* help him and that there needed to be a balance with my intervening. Allowing him the space to navigate challenges would enable him to grow, and it was going to catapult him forward.

This is true for all of us.

It's easier to avoid new activities and to shy away from challenges and activities that push us out of our comfort zone. But not tryng new things holds us back. It keeps us from growing and thriving. The words we speak to our kids become the ceiling we place over their heads. They will always work until they meet that ceiling, and in order to penetrate that ceiling placed on their heads, they will need to do some internal work when they grow up. Our words transpire to become a barrier keeping them from what they can do, who they can become, and their belief in themselves in achieving what might seem challenging.

The way we speak to our children, regardless of their ability level, puts them on a spectrum that ranges from limitless to confined.

Max felt limitless because we never told him he wasn't. We never spoke to him in a way that limited his own belief in himself. He could always do anything he wanted so long as he was safe, and it pulled so much inspiration from his own soul to do just that as he grew up.

It would have been easier for him not to try to do new activities, but we never wanted to hold him back. It was a great lesson to us in how we speak with our children. Max didn't know he was different, and we wanted to keep it that way. We were intentional with our words and our actions every day so we could make sure that he never felt like he couldn't do something. Our rallying cry in those early years was that we (and Max) could do all things through Christ. There were no limitations. He surprised us daily by learning something new and wanting to try a new activity. He was boundless energy and joy, and we loved it. This was a blessing, and it was what we constantly prayed for as he grew.

When Max was two years old, our daughter Madeline was born. The trauma of what we went through with Max lingered in our minds like smoke on water. We had struggled with going through the process of pregnancy and delivery again. Although the doctors told us how rare it was to have this happen again, we were anxious. Even so, we wanted to have another child close in age so they could help one another and learn from one another as they each developed skills. This was only going to bring Max and the whole family forward in a positive way.

The moment Madeline was born, all our fears or concerns disappeared. She and Max had a special relationship from the start. Having them so close in age was a blessing as they learned and grew together. Sometimes Madeline would do things before Max, but they didn't care as long as Max was doing it too.

By the time Max was three years old, he was going to occupational therapy, physical therapy, and speech therapy three times a week. My friends were taking their toddlers to park playdates and story time, and it felt like we were always taking Max to another appointment. But this was our journey, and we were called to do it. We were proactive and put everything we could into supporting Max, and we wouldn't have had it any other way. It was simply different paths.

I decided early into those appointments that if this was our world, I would make it shine. I turned those therapists into friends and went out of my way to build relationships with them. They weren't just another person—they were a part of our family as they supported Max's development.

One therapist, Orlynn, introduced me to a church community where we could thrive. There's no way that wasn't God's hand in our lives, directing us to that therapist and inspiring her to tell us about that church. It changed us, and we changed it.

When I arrived at the church, I instantly loved the people and the welcoming spirit. But there wasn't a mom's group or anything to support mothers of young children. I personally needed and wanted it most, and I figured other moms needed it too. So, I started a mom's morning out group where mothers could bring their children, fellowship with each other, and support each other through their own journey of motherhood.

It was life-changing, not only for me but for all who joined the group. It pushed me to build the right relationships, and those relationships pushed me to participate in other activities, and those activities inspired me to create a community for other mothers just like me.

The paths each of us take vary, but they are all with purpose. Each and every one of us has a path we are destined to walk down, and as long as we walk with it rather than resist it, beautiful blessings will bloom.

As I write this, that group has grown into a large Christian school with 250 graduates. It has impacted the lives of hundreds of mothers and children, and it continues to thrive as the years go on. And so did our family. What began as angst and unknown in the hospital just a few years earlier began blossoming into one of our greatest blessings. Yes, it was busy and chaotic as we acclimated as new parents, but it was beautiful simply because we chose to focus on the beauty of our situation. That alone made all the difference.

What could have been viewed as a challenging time of parenting brought us incredible joy. Sometimes, we simply have to trust the process. Many times, things make little sense. It's challenging to understand why things happen the way they do when we are in the moment.

But so long as you trust God, it will become clear years down the line why something is happening in the present day. Our struggles will all make sense one day as long as we keep moving forward with the right attitude. Once we see life in enlightened hindsight, we'll praise God in gratitude for the challenges we went through.

Chapter 8 | No Limitations

Stephanie

> *"For we live by faith, not by sight."*
> —2 Corinthians 5:7 (NIV)

Before Max was born, I had prepared myself for the many roles of a mother: comforter, teacher, and protector. But I hadn't realized what would become one of my most important roles for Max—an advocate.

As Max grew into a rambunctious child, his energy was infectious. We wanted the world for him, but the world often couldn't see beyond his disabilities. My job was to stand up for Max and ensure he had the best opportunities, all while guided by God's grace.

That advocacy started early as Max approached school age. As my friends and other parents in the area began planning where to send their children to school, Stephen and I had serious conversations about what school would look like for Max and where he needed to go. Many parents in similar situations isolate their children and send them to specialized schools. We felt strongly that Max needed the experience of attending a school that welcomed all types of students, not just those with disabilities, but the idea of dropping our sweet boy at a school where he would stand out was terrifying.

We were nervous as we approached the decision, but we didn't need to be. As he had been before, God was there, seeing us through every step of the way.

We started Max in a kindergarten class where he was integrated with all the kids. The beautiful thing was that when the kids saw that something was different about Max, they didn't care. Young children are so Christ-like in their love and acceptance that they welcomed Max with open arms. But we weren't sure it was the right fit for Max, so after that school year and every other year, we carefully—and prayerfully evaluated where Max should go next. We tried him in public, Montessori, and private schools to find the right fit for his learning style.

Every year was a fresh start, which meant new opportunities for Max. It also meant more roadblocks and battles for me. We were faced with countless meetings, paperwork, and academic plans to sort through, and people would often tell me how to act or what to decide. At first, it was easier just to listen to what they had to say and follow their guidance as they put our son into a box. But that wasn't always getting us the results we wanted or putting Max in the best place to succeed. The experts at the school did their best, but they would always put our son in a box. He had disabilities—that was it for them. They couldn't see past it, and their recommendations would reflect that.

I soon learned to respond, "Wait a minute here, I'm the mother!" I had every right to stand up for myself and advocate for Max. In fact, that was my God-given responsibility. I had to embrace the warrior mentality to stand up for Max and do what I knew was best for him as his mother.

Over Max's elementary years, we had numerous IEP meetings to discuss his learning needs and the best situation and resources for Max to learn and develop. Not a single IEP meeting went by that I didn't start with a prayer—vocally, so the teachers and school administrators could hear and participate. I needed God in that room, and I wanted everyone to know that He was there. And as I called on the Lord, He gave me wisdom and discernment to overcome every challenge and roadblock. I knew I was Max's advocate and would never stop pushing. There were no limits on Max, and I had to make sure the schools saw it that way as well. We had to make things happen for Max.

Some people sometimes viewed me as overbearing, but I knew what I needed to do. I relied on the Holy Spirit and looked straight ahead. I would speak up and fight for what I wanted with grace and class, but I was not stopping until I got what I knew was right for my son. Max deserved that.

In life, we often face distractions from doing what we know is right and what we need to do. We may feel pressured to take a certain path or pulled away from what we know is the best choice if we listen too much to what others want us to do. I felt that as we moved through Max's schooling—everyone had an opinion, but so many of their ideas were just noise that pulled me away from following what the Lord said was best for Max. We can feel those pulls and distractions in every decision we make: where to go to school, where to live, what job to take, and how to worship.

We have to trust God, focus on what matters, and cut through the noise and distractions to do what the Lord wants us to do. We have to look straight ahead to what matters rather than allow other people's ideas and influences to pull us off course. We became warriors for Max, powered by prayer to stand up for him and put him in the best place possible.

As I was facing challenges in school meetings and principals' offices, Max was overcoming challenges on his own. He was determined to push through those challenges and find ways to thrive on his own terms—just like his mama. We were both tenaciously pursuing the best-case scenario for his situation, and it was amazing to see him champion himself just as I was doing for him in the background. Max was resilient. No matter what was happening behind the scenes, Max worked hard and always had a smile on his face.

At this point, Max attended an elementary school with an integrated program that allowed him to be surrounded by students of all abilities. Through this, his biggest challenges were unveiled. It wasn't anything in the classroom; he was catching on to concepts and learning. It was his social skills. The friendliness of his kindergarten class changed as the kids got older.

Birthday invitations would be sent to all the kids except for Max. Kids would play with each other and leave him out. It was heartbreaking to see this happen, just because other kids saw him as different. We tried so hard to get Max to see himself as no different from any other kid, but the kids at school didn't see it that way.

I couldn't be in the classroom with Max, but I could have the best attitude for him. My mantra became, "We're going to make this happen." I didn't get caught up in support groups where parents dwelled on their children's differences and displayed their "woe-is-me" attitude. I was too busy encouraging Max and finding him the best places to thrive.

It felt bigger than me. It felt bigger than just our family. I knew Max could leave an imprint on this world and on the lives of many, and I had to honor that calling from the Lord. And so we continued on, day by day, introducing him to new things that could broaden his perspective.

Outside of school, Max started horseback riding. The idea was terrifying to me as a mother—I was supposed to sit back while my tiny son sat on that huge, powerful animal? We still did it. Fear had no place in our minds, we were walking entirely by faith. I knew that this was what we needed to do, and I wanted to make sure Max knew he could do anything he wanted to. We would support him in every hobby and activity he wanted to try, even if I had to sit on the sidelines and watch through fingers closed over my eyes praying under my breath.

Horseback riding ended up being the perfect activity for Max. He loved spending time with those beautiful animals and learned balance and confidence as his skills grew. Even though he was just five years old when he started, it was amazing watching Max go from a timid young boy on the horse to a confident rider. He even ended up winning a few horse shows, and the owners of the barn threw him a big birthday party. After years of not getting invited to birthday parties for the kids at school, seeing Max's face light up as he entered the barn full of balloons and happy faces was priceless.

The initial hesitation of putting him in horseback riding evolved into a new community full of love and joy. Max couldn't stop smiling when he was around the horses, and that joy spread to all of us. Horseback riding did more than just give Max something to do after school—it strengthened our souls and surrounded us with a community of loving, beautiful people.

He was shining his light on horseback, and we wanted Max to continue to shine in school and beyond. We continued to move Max to different schools. When he hit third grade, we realized he needed something bigger and different from what he had experienced before. He needed the social aspect as much as the academic.

We had solved the puzzle of what Max needed to thrive and be his true self. When he was his truest self, his light shined the brightest. And as we dialed in on how to help let that truth out of him, everything shifted.

Chapter 9 | Growing Up

Stephanie

> *"In all these things we are more than conquerors through him who loved us."*
>
> *—Romans 8:37 (NIV)*

The years went on, and we welcomed the stereotypical teenage years that all parents worry about. As we nervously approached that bridge, we looked at Max with excitement. We knew that what lay ahead would be amazing to watch so long as we supported him to grow into his own and let his light shine.

All his life, we had been planting seeds that gave Max the confidence and support to thrive.

When Max was ten years old, we decided to move to Greenville, South Carolina, so Max could attend Hidden Treasures Christian School. Unlike some schools that wanted to hide kids with special needs, Hidden Treasures was founded on the core belief that children are born with hidden treasures. That's how we have always treated Max: like the treasure from God that he is.

It was a busy time for our family with Max moving to a new school, Stephen getting his MBA at night, and me starting my skincare company. But we each knew we were where we needed to be. Even with more demands on my time than before, Max was still my top priority. Being his mom and advocating for and supporting him was what God needed me to be.

We continued encouraging Max to try new activities, and he chose tae kwon do. He jumped in with his usual enthusiasm. We knew he would be great, but some of the instructors were skeptical about having Max in their class. I chalked it up to simply a lack of understanding. I couldn't be mad at those who were skeptical, whether tae kwon do or another activity. It was new. It was foreign to them. They didn't know what they didn't know, and that resulted in skepticism and hesitation when accepting a child like Max into their program.

My respect and admiration go out to those who walk in faith toward something new. The instructors at this tae kwon do studio had just that. And it helped that Max brought his resilient and positive attitude to the mix. Max won them over with his incredible love and hard work. He brought a light to each instructor and showed them who he truly was. The first test came to advance his belt. He performed what he was taught over the previous month or two and showcased his formations to the instructor. At the end of the test, the instructor awarded him with his new belt as tears strolled down their faces.

Their overwhelm came from the abundant love they felt from my boy. Max brought purpose to their work, and it showed. Max wasn't just there to take his test like every other student; he was there to make a new friend. He was there to help the instructors have a better day. He was there to bring positive energy to every person who walked through the doors of that studio. With each belt, the instructors became more and more attached to Max's journey. He made it nearly to a black belt, and the experience not only changed Max's life, but it changed the lives of the instructors who taught him.

Tae kwon do blessed Max. It taught him focus, respect, and motivation. But those blessings went both ways: Max blessed his teachers with so much love and enthusiasm. In everything Max did, he brought tremendous love and joy to those around him. He spread his light and love of Christ to every person he met, and his influence grew.

Max was light and love everywhere he went. But even as a teenager, we still struggled with where to send him to high school. Would he be in a loving environment? Would he be bullied? All these questions fluttered my mind, and I wanted to protect him from that negativity just as I had done all his life.

So, I prayed. I understood that God's protection was with him, and it brought me comfort to know that as long as our decision was rooted in love and faith, we wouldn't be led astray. We settled on sending him to high school with his sister at the private Catholic school next door. We felt good about our decision, but it didn't make the start of high school any easier.

Freshman and sophomore years were a challenge. It was hard to watch our son struggle in a new environment and to find his community at school when we knew he had so much love to give. It was as if we were standing on the other side of a locked door holding the key. We knew how to get in, but we couldn't reach the other side to hand the key to the people who were locked out.

While we waited for things to change, we prayed. We hoped to God that Max would come out of his shell and touch the lives of his classmates and teachers, showing them who he was and what he was capable of. After countless prayers, things turned around in his third year.

Max and Stephen became managers of the school's soccer team. Soccer was huge at this school. To have Max leading the team allowed him to influence countless people. In his role as manager, Max blossomed and showed off his strengths. He made the announcements for the soccer team and was involved in every aspect of the game.

Max excelled in his role. He genuinely loved each person on the team and took the time to build relationships with them. He used his God-given wit and outgoing nature to minister to the players and coaches and show them all things are possible. It was this experience that allowed Max to grow into himself and allow his authenticity to shine. He shared his light and love with each player on the team, and those friendships blossomed off the field as Max sat with the team at lunch and told jokes.

They could see that Max was a light. He brought positivity and love to every interaction, and it was reciprocated once it was realized. It was beautiful to see other people witnessing the love and charisma I had always known Max had.

Max came out of his shell with the soccer team. It was all the Lord in him, encouraging Max to go out of his way to make those friendships. After a rough start to high school, Max needed friends. And they needed him.

I could see the change happening in the soccer team because of Max, and I knew God wanted the world to see it, too. We prayed as a family how to share

Max's story. The answer came: I needed to call News 4 to have them highlight how Max was changing lives. People often are not comfortable around people with special needs because they don't know how to act. I knew I had to share Max's story so people realized he was incredible, bright, and social, just like many other kids. The more it was normalized, the more space there would be for Max and kids like Max.

The news crew was scheduled to come to a big soccer game, film Max, and interview him and some of the players. But leading up to the big day, we watched as the weather reports started predicting a major storm was coming our way—potentially delaying or canceling the game and the story. I prayed so hard that the sun would shine so the world could learn about Max. Within an hour of my prayer, the clouds broke, and the sun began to shine. The game went on as scheduled, and the news crew arrived.

Max's story soon hit the airwaves, just like God wanted it to. It was a beautifully compiled story that exhibited the camaraderie of the team, the tenacity of the soccer organization, and above all, the miracle that carried the team through to win the championship: Max.

Max spent six years in high school, and he spent four years helping manage the soccer team. Every year of those four years, the team went to the state championship. Of those four, they won the title twice, crowning their school as the state champions.

We never could have predicted the miraculous impact soccer would have on Max. It was the turning point of Max's evolution in high school as he gained the confidence to spread his wings and transform the community.

Max had always been an encourager. He's real with people and doesn't see labels or social status, just people to love. That pure love and energy were fresh air for those high schoolers. Max loved them with no agenda or hidden meaning. He would go up to each player and say, "I love you, you're a great guy," or text them in the middle of the night telling them he loves them. That's just Max being Max, sharing his love and light with others. And it brought meaning and love to those kids when they needed it in their confusing teenage years.

His final season concluded as we attended the team banquet, and the coaches recognized Max, and at the end of their sentiments, the entire room stood. The team had won the state championship, but they gave Max a standing ovation because of the love and care he showed each of them.

All the trials of his early years were worth it to see Max shine in that moment. Everything we had poured into our son, all the patience, the effort, the love, and the lessons we had given him—it was as if it was all manifested in that moment. It was at this point that Max realized what he was capable of. His face lit up, and he waved with joy to the entire soccer organization as they cheered and applauded. He saw his light and love reciprocated on a large scale, and it was as if someone added fuel to his fire.

Even now, Max is still in touch with those soccer players years later. The bond they built can't be broken. But it wasn't just soccer. Throughout high school, Max continued to shine in other areas, too. He was finding his place and realizing the light and joy he could bring to others.

A family in our neighborhood asked Max to help with the bible study they taught at the Brookwood Church in town. Max enthusiastically agreed and was assigned to the class of fourth graders. Of course, they instantly fell in love with Max. Max loved them right back with his trademark smile and care. Word of Max's sweet spirit traveled quickly around the church, and soon Max was MC'ing events and stealing the show. Everyone from the band members to the little kids who attended bible study loved him. Max was nothing short of a church celebrity.

Because of Brookwood's commitment to the special needs community, they partnered with Tim Tebow Night to Shine Prom for the debut of Night to Shine, a special needs prom. As with anything new, there's always uncertainty about whether it will succeed. Would there even be an interest in this? Would we have people attend, or would we be spinning our wheels to plan a big event for a small turnout?

It blew our doubts out of the water. Nearly 1,000 special needs guests showed up in their prom ensembles, and 1,500 people volunteered—including Tim Tebow, who flew in for the event.

Max turned Brookwood around with his love and good energy. Everyone he ran into would get an exuberant high five. His positive actions built a strong community and he became beloved around the church and town. His infectious, God-given energy warms everyone he comes in contact with.

As with every teenager, graduating from high school is a major milestone. Max hit that mark when he was twenty when he and Madeline graduated the same year. It was a major blessing in his life and a turning point. We had a general idea of what his life would be like through elementary, middle, and high school. Graduation was the culmination of years of work for me and Max. It was also a turning point as we entered the unknown—what would Max do next? How would he find his place outside high school?

We learned that no matter the circumstances, people matter most. Life is about connection. Without a deeply connected community and Max's natural ability to unite people, the high school years would have been much more difficult. Max left a major imprint on the community with a lasting influence.

As each of us walks through this life, we have a vision or a hope of how things will play out. You have an idea of the future, and it can change in an instant. Many coil at the thought of the unknown, allowing change to bring in anxiety and doubt. But when you walk in faith and trust what it is the lord has planned, you find comfort. And one day, you look back to understand exactly why things played out the way that they did. What once felt out of your control becomes familiar, and you realize it all happened for a greater purpose than you can imagine.

Chapter 10 | The Impact on Each Other

Madeline

"This is how God showed his love among us:
He sent his one and only Son into the world
that we might live through him.
This is love: not that we loved God,
but that he loved us and sent his Son
as an atoning sacrifice for our sins."
—*1 John 4:9-10 (NIV)*

We were downtown, a day like any other. Everything was fine until we walked back to our car to realize that it was being towed. I was still very young, and Max—oh, dear Max—he sprung into a full tae kwon do mode, ready to defend our family car against the tow guys.

My emotions danced between amusement, awe, and a tinge that our car would be gone for good. It was a moment that, in retrospect, captured the spirit of my brother: fiercely protective, adorably uninhibited, and always unpredictable.

As a small child, I never knew that Max was any different from anyone else. We shared the same friend group, enjoyed the same movies and shows (like *Toy Story*, *Tarzan*, and *Barney*), and even had similar tastes in food. The only difference I noticed was during dress-up; he loved being a firefighter while I embraced my inner ballerina.

Back then, it didn't occur to me that Max was different in any way. The realization of his uniqueness hit me when others began pointing it out. People would ask questions like, "Why does your brother talk funny?" and "Why does he drool? Why does he still wear pull-ups?"

Once I was asked those questions, I began to wonder about the answers myself. These questions confused me—Max's way of speaking made perfect sense to me, and his habits were just part of who he was. Max was just . . . Max. I began to wonder, was Max really different? I couldn't quite grasp it.

It wasn't until second or third grade that I started to see it for myself. Max suddenly wasn't a perfect fit with my friend group, and our play styles and humor weren't in harmony as they once were. It was a confusing time, leading me to approach my mom with my questions.

She explained gently that Max was born with mild cerebral palsy, a condition that set him on a distinct journey. While he faced unique challenges, he was, at the core, no different from anyone else. As I grappled with this revelation, the world was quick to remind me of our differences.

Kids can be harsh, and their cruelty stung. I used to include Max when my friends visited, but over time, they pulled away—yet I realized that those people who distanced themselves were individuals I didn't need in my life. It was a pivotal lesson that extended beyond Max's condition; it showed me the true value of authentic friendships.

Despite the challenges, I never held Max responsible for any of it. How could I? He was my brother, and his uniqueness was an integral part of our shared journey. It was during this time that I recognized I, too, would always stand out because of my brother with special needs.

As the years rolled on, my choices and opportunities were guided by the need to accommodate Max's well-being. No driving a car or pursuing distant colleges— these limitations were sacrifices I willingly made to ensure Max's inclusion and comfort. Yet, through it all, Max emerged as a beacon of inspiration. His presence and his unwavering faith inspired not just me, but many around him.

By the time we were teenagers, the world had firmly placed its lens over my eyes, and I could see the divide widening. While he had once fit seamlessly into my circle, now the jokes, the games, and the conversations seemed to veer away from him. It was heartbreaking, but it also birthed resilience. When so-called friends distanced themselves because of Max, they distilled my life, leaving behind only the genuine, kind-hearted souls I could rely on. It was a lesson not just about my brother, but about life's larger truths: the worth of authenticity and the unimportance of superficiality.

Throughout the years, as a teenager and young adult, I consciously made choices that would never dim his light. And now, in our adulthood, we have embraced our individuality—recognizing that it's absolutely okay to be different. That our differences complement each other perfectly.

Our paths have evolved as we have grown. It's no longer about restraining ourselves to elevate the other; I've come to realize that our differences are our strengths. Today, it's clear that Max's journey is one that touches hearts and fosters a belief in something greater. It inspires the deepest parts within us to lean into our differences and pursue that which makes us unique from others.

It just might be the secret to making an impact in this world.

Chapter 11 | What Makes You Different?

Stephanie

God works in different ways, but it is the same God who does the work in all of us.

—1 Corinthians 12:6 (NLT)

Stephen and I often set aside personal ambitions and dreams to ensure Max's well-being. We knew the path wouldn't be easy, but with God's grace, we were determined to journey through it together. Our family bond was our strength—the glue that held us together through the rough patches.

When it came time for Max to graduate from high school, my heart swelled. I found myself battling contrasting emotions. Riding high on his accomplishments and his entrance into the world as a young man, and also the anxiety about what the future might hold for him. High school graduation is a rite of passage for many, a threshold to new beginnings.

Most of his peers were gearing up for college, trade schools, or diving into their careers. Yet, for children with special needs, the transition can be a challenging one. The routines they've grown accustomed to, the friends they've made—it all shifts, and they're faced with a new world of responsibilities that they don't always understand.

Stephen and I poured our souls into giving Max the best life, and as this chapter drew to a close, we were fervently praying for guidance on the next steps. We knew he had so much to offer the world, and the thought of him losing that spark was unimaginable. Raising a child with unique needs meant everyday decisions carried more weight. Every milestone, birthday, and even ordinary days were filled with questions: *Are we accommodating Max enough? Does he feel included and cherished? How can we reiterate to him that he has no limits, no matter his circumstances?* And each time these thoughts weighed on our hearts, we would pray. We would seek guidance and comfort, and ask God to be with us as we made these impactful decisions with and for Max.

God's grace was our constant companion, guiding us when the path became foggy, and lifting us when our spirits waned. As years passed, this journey knitted our family tighter. The shared experiences, challenges, laughter, and tears built an unbreakable bond between the four of us.

It was during this phase that our daughter decided on Furman University for her own journey. As she transitioned to her new academic life, she became Max's beacon of inspiration. I could see the pride in her eyes every time she spoke of her brother. Her love for Max led her to an organization called Best Buddies International. It was as if God had directed her steps toward this organization that focused on integrating young adults with special needs into society.

Embracing the mission of Best Buddies, she and Max initiated a chapter at Furman University. And in a twist of serendipity, Stephen took up the role of area director for Best Buddies in South Carolina.

Our family had found another purpose, another calling, and it was all by leaning into what made our family's story so unique. Max's journey and the challenges he faced were now opening doors for others like him.

Best Buddies was not just another organization; it was a movement. A movement to shift perceptions, to highlight the gifts and potential of those with special needs. Max became an ambassador of Best Buddies, and he swayed and moved audiences with his authentic charm.

I watched as Max addressed crowds, and broke barriers, my heart swelled with pride. Here was my son, a testament to what love, faith, and perseverance could achieve. And he was sharing with the world with the help of his loving sister and father.

Word spread like wildfire about the Best Buddies chapter at Furman. Our daughter's friends and even strangers from across the campus were drawn to its mission. Together, they raised awareness, shattered misconceptions, and redefined possibilities for people

with special needs. They were not just changing minds; they were touching souls.

It was in this season of our lives that I had a profound realization. It wasn't just Max who stood out because of his unique challenges. Each of us, in our own way, had been shaped by our experiences with him. His journey had molded our perspectives and made us more compassionate, more patient, and more resilient. *His* journey brought us purpose and passion.

Life has a way of teaching us lessons in the most unexpected ways. Max's life teaches us about the beauty within our differences. We all have our strengths, our quirks, and our unique attributes. But these differences, instead of setting us apart, bring us together. They make us human. They make us real. And when we lean into those differences, we are really leaning into our gifts. Our purpose.

It's easy to fall into the trap of comparing ourselves to some perceived notion of "normal." But the truth is, every single person is different from the next. It's these very differences that are our superpowers. When we embrace our individuality and lean into our unique strengths, we create ripples of change that can transform families, communities, and yes, even the world.

Max's journey, filled with its ups and downs, is a testament to the power of love, faith, and acceptance. I often find myself reflecting on our journey, filled with gratitude for the lessons we have learned. And as we walk hand in hand into the future, I am reminded of a truth that anchors our family: it's not just okay to be different—it's a blessing. Our unique attributes complement each other, weaving a tapestry of love, strength, and hope. And with God's grace guiding us, I truly believe the best is yet to come.

To learn more about Best Buddies,
scan the QR code below.

Chapter 12 | God's Plan

Stephen

"In fact, we expected to die. But as a result, we stopped relying on ourselves and learned to rely only on God, who raises the dead."

—*2 Corinthians 1:9 (NLT)*

We all want to love and to be loved.

We all want to live a life of purpose and passion.

And we all want our time in this life to be one that leaves a mark.

I truly believe our faith in God enabled Stephanie, Madeline, Max, and myself to step into realizing those blessings. Of course, it came with difficulty. It was nothing short of challenging. We struggled through many days, wondered about God's plan, and went through the deep emotions that came with the trials of the journey. But we never questioned what was happening. We wondered why, but we never lost faith that it was for a purpose greater than us.

Things were falling into place as our children grew. They found new passions and discovered their purpose as they lived each day. Time went on, and everything was in flow. The Lord blessed us to see clearly what we needed to do as a family.

In the blink of an eye, Stephanie and I had two young adult children. We sat together and reminisced about the early days when both the kids were in diapers. We were getting our feet under us as parents, navigating what was already a difficult experience with an added layer of complexity given Max's circumstances. And we rose to the occasion—together.

We persevered, stayed motivated, and dreamed of what could be. This was just as true from when we first met and pursued our careers to when we became parents and built a family.

We supported each other.

We were there for each other.

When times got hard, we leaned on each other, each of us pulling an incomparable strength from the Lord.

We believed that Jesus had a hand in everything. In every moment. Even when it didn't make sense to us.

From the moment we sat in the emergency waiting room before Stephanie was whisked back for an emergency C-section to the moment we watched Max and Madeline command a room and bring joy to their community while doing deeply meaningful work, we never lost that faith. But then tragedy hit again.

I was transitioning from one work opportunity to another when I started feeling sick and tired. A trip to the emergency room determined my hemoglobin level was at 3.6. Normally these levels are at 15. That day, I was diagnosed with PRCA.

We wrestled with the diagnosis—hadn't we already faced enough trials?

After a month of PCRA treatment, things got even worse.

I started having headaches so severe they had to be treated with prescription painkillers.

It went on like this for weeks with no relief. Finally, the doctors sent me for a CT scan. We just needed answers, something that could help us understand the issue and resolve it. But the scan came back normal.

We were baffled.

Seeing my struggles and total exhaustion, Stephanie jumped into her fixer mode. She wanted to do everything in her power to make sure I didn't have to suffer longer than necessary. We would find the best treatment as quickly as possible and bring me comfort and relief.

It was a blessing when we learned that a leading treatment was available nearby at Duke University in Durham, North Carolina. It seemed like our only option, but it was risky. I would receive IVs of ATG horse serum to kill specific cells in my immune system that were attacking bone marrow stem cells. The treatment would help my body rebuild its supply of bone marrow stem cells, causing blood counts to go up.[3]

It was the best choice remaining, so the next Sunday, I went to the pastor and was anointed with the same oil given to us for Max.

It reminded us of a scripture found in James 5:14-16:

> *Is anyone among you sick? Let them call the elders of the church to pray over them and anoint them with oil in the name of the Lord. And the prayer offered in faith will make the sick person well; the Lord will raise them up. If they have sinned, they will be forgiven. Therefore confess your sins to each other and pray for each other so that you may be healed. The prayer of a righteous person is powerful and effective.*

The pastor gave me a simple but heartfelt prayer. We were still nervous about the procedure but felt comforted by the healing power of Christ.

My procedure was the next day, and Stephanie was heartbroken that she couldn't make it to be by my side because she was working extra hours. For that reason, we planned for the assisting pastor, who was

---

3   https://www.aamds.org/diseases/related/pure-red-cell-aplasia-prca

an absolute angel, to drive me over three hours to the procedure in Durham.

But on the drive to the procedure, I could tell something was wrong. It was more than just the general illness and fatigue of the previous weeks. I needed to get to the hospital as fast as possible.

When I arrived at Duke, I rushed to the appointment area, sat, and waited. Suddenly, I became disoriented and collapsed to the floor with a massive seizure. Praise God I was in the right place at the right time.

Over the rest of the day, I had five more seizures. I was supposed to be going in for a relatively simple procedure and ended up in intensive care. Stephanie got the call, and she, Max, and her dad traveled to Duke.

We had no idea whether the stroke was related to my PRCA diagnosis or another cause. A cloud of uncertainty and fear hung over our family.

This feeling was familiar.

Chapter 13 | Faith Over Fear

Stephanie

*"Praise be to the God and Father of our
Lord Jesus Christ, the Father of compassion
and the God of all comfort, who comforts us
in all our troubles, so that we can comfort
those in any trouble with the comfort we
ourselves receive from God."*

—2 Corinthians 1:3-4 (NIV)

*"God is our refuge and strength,
an ever-present help in trouble."*

—Psalm 46:1 (NIV)

Our first evening in Durham, left my father and I
totally exhausted—physically and mentally. The
drive and emotional toll of being back in the hospital
wiped us out, so we returned to the hotel. Stephen
assured us he was fine and in the best hands.

But around three a.m., I received a phone call. It was a nurse from the hospital telling me that Stephen had suffered a massive stroke. I sat there in shock. Every ounce of hope drained from my body as I took in the news.

The doctors in South Carolina had done scans recently and hadn't seen anything concerning. How did they miss the warning signs for a stroke? Would Stephen make it through the night and be okay?

In that dark hotel room, my tough demeanor cracked. I felt broken.

I try to be strong for everyone else, but this felt like too much to handle. We had already been down a similar road with Max. I couldn't bear the thought of doing something similar with my husband.

As tears rolled down my cheeks and my heart sank deeper and deeper into the fear of losing my beloved husband, I felt something move next to me. I looked over, and I saw Max. He was wide awake, sitting right by my side. He looked right at me with a deep, harrowing look in his eyes as he rubbed my back.

"It's going to be okay," he said in a calm, sweet voice.

He didn't know what had happened to his dad. All he knew was that I needed strength and faith.

At that moment, we all got up, got dressed, and rushed back to the hospital. Hours and hours passed as we sat in the waiting room awaiting an answer. We weren't sure what the outcome would be as we camped in the hospital.

The unknown was terrifying. This feeling felt familiar.

I had met this worry before. And the last time it came, I fought tooth and nail in every moment thereafter for the next twenty-two years to balance it and bring a sense of "normal."

I kept losing myself in the thought of the worst-case scenario. Will I have to do this life alone? Will I have to take care of both Stephen and Max? What is going to happen?

And as I slouched down into my chair, head in hand, I cried. And every time I would feel this low, a warm hand would go to my back and tell me everything was going to be okay.

Max.

Every moment I would lose myself to fear, Max would instill faith. He would pray with me, he would sit with me, he would hope with me. And he wouldn't leave my side through it all.

"It's going to be okay, Mom," he would continuously say in a calm and sweet voice.

In that moment, I had a flashback to the moment Stephen told me those exact same words on our drive to the hospital when Max was born.

And at that moment, I knew it was going to be okay. Stephen was going to be okay. We were going to be okay.

Right then, the doctor came out to the waiting room to let us know what had occurred.

His red blood cells were low, and his body wasn't processing and receiving oxygen.

He had a severe cerebral venous thrombosis stroke due to a lack of oxygen to his brain. As a result, Stephen suffered a traumatic brain injury.

In those days in the hospital, just as we had experienced when Max was born twenty-two years before, we saw countless miracles. We prayed and worked on his recovery. Through God's grace, Stephen slowly made a full recovery.

From the moment it all started, I could feel Max's calm energy. He comforted me in a time that felt so out of our control.

The miracle had come full circle.

Chapter 14 | Believe in Miracles

Stephanie

*"Now to him who is able to do
immeasurably more than all we ask or
imagine, according to His power that is at
work within us."*

—*Ephesians 3:20 (NIV)*

Watching Max grow into a thriving adult has been the biggest blessing of my life. But the miracles haven't stopped. As I write this book, Max is a staple in our community.

In 2015, Max started working with a personal trainer, who quickly realized Max would do an incredible job working at the Sports Club front desk. He is truly in his element as he welcomes people, answers questions, and is the smiling face everyone sees when they walk in the door. Everyone in town knows and loves him. Their love and support have changed Max's life as he lifts and brightens theirs.

In 2019, when Max was twenty-five, he decided to be freshwater baptized. It was a beautiful day, and the sun shined down on us all, warming our skin and our hearts as we walked into the outdoor amphitheater.

Max was surrounded by many relatives, friends from church, and friends and community members from the Sports Club. As Max rose from the water, his smile reached every corner of the sky.

It felt like he was shining with the light of Christ.

Max is doing God's work daily and has helped grow the special needs program at the church to more than 150 families. Many of these families are in similar situations to where we were years ago: navigating the complicated and unknown path of having a child with special needs. Max is there to offer the support we often didn't have and to love them on that journey with the help of God and the community Max created. These families and kids look up to Max, see all the love and positivity he has brought to the world, and realize they can follow in his footsteps.

As I've shared Max's story, some people have told me that the miracles we have received seem too big for their "smaller" challenges. But it's not the size or intensity of our struggles that matter. We all face battles. Christ's light and guidance are available to everyone.

Our attitude and relationship with Christ can get us through any trial or tribulation, big or small. We have faced challenges over the last thirty years beyond what I could imagine, but Christ has steered us through them all.

Christ is everything.

I've learned that nothing is perfect, except God. I pray for His wisdom, strength, and grace every day. People often see the poised woman working through challenges, but they don't see the struggles, pleading prayers, and family support behind the scenes.

Through God's grace, I've had the strength to show up and fight for Max every day. My relationship with Jesus is the most precious thing in my life because it has given me everything—especially my family.

I've felt God's love in hospital rooms where I've seen visions and heard his voice. But I've also felt his love through a hug from a friend, the words to say in a tense meeting to get Max into the right school, and the bright smile from Max after a long day.

There are no guarantees in life. Every day is a gift, and you have to be a fighter to make it through challenges with a positive attitude. My rallying cry for years has been Philippians 4:13: *I can do all this through him who gives me strength.*

Ever since the day Max was born, I knew we would have to walk through trials and that people wouldn't understand him. But I knew we could endure and thrive with the strength of Christ. We can do all things. That faith and belief helped us through unbelievable challenges.

But Christ's strength isn't limited to major trials or life-changing ordeals. No matter what you're dealing with, however big or small it may seem, Christ's strength makes it possible to do *all* things. His strength and love are the foundation for our hard work and positivity to make miracles happen.

When you invite Him in, He comes in.
When we believe, we receive.

We wouldn't have received such glorious blessings if I didn't believe in Christ's miracles and persevere with his strength every day. That belief and those blessings are not what we expected, but they are available to us all.

Max is a miracle, and he has brought incredible miracles and blessings into our lives and the entire community. When I look back at who I was as a newlywed and expectant mother, I could never have imagined the road our family would be on. We have faced countless trials, challenges, and storms in life. But those trials have taught us to surrender and focus on Jesus. With faith and perseverance, the storms cease and turn into blessings.

Life didn't go how we expected or planned, but what we received is greater than anything we could do on our own. Being Max's parents is our own trip to Holland. As we believe, we receive. And we've received an incredible blessing from Max.

No matter your circumstances or the twists and turns in your life, Christ's life and guidance is always there. His love is available to everyone and can turn even what may seem the largest trials into the biggest miracles and blessings.

Supporting Materials

Consider reflecting on this story for your own growth.

1. What part of Max's story gives you hope?

2. What challenge have you faced that felt bigger than you could handle?

3. Who do you trust to guide you through the challenges of life?

4. If God is listening, what would you want to say to Him?

5. Read the verse below. How does the claim of the Bible verse John 3:16 affect you?

"For God so loved the world that he gave his one and only Son, that whoever believes in him shall not perish but have eternal life."

—John 3:16 (NIV)

Stay Connected

Get Involved in Set Free Alliance

The McChesney's are proud to support the work of the **Set Free Alliance**. This nonprofit organization is committed to rescuing, healing, giving clean water, and discipleship through transforming entire villages by drilling a water well, rescuing children from slavery, providing medical aid, and establishing churches in India.

Find out more about this powerful, impactful organization and how you can also help by scanning this QR code:

Learn more about Tim Tebow's Night to Shine

Night to Shine is a complimentary event for people with special needs hosted by local churches around the world. The event is open to anyone living with disabilities, ages fourteen and older. Although each event is a bit different, some activities included are a red carpet entrance, limousine rides, dancing, karaoke, gifts, a catered dinner, a Respite Room for parents and caregivers, a crowning ceremony where every honored guest will receive a crown or tiara, and more—Night to Shine is a celebration of God's love for YOU, our Kings and Queens!

To attend Night to Shine as an honored guest, you will register through your local host church location, and once registered, your local host location will provide all necessary information to you about attending Night to Shine.

"Our salvation, and the work that we have been divinely prepared for, was established in love according to His eternal purpose. And now, through the church, and with his power we are called to know this love and lead with this love, to fulfill His purpose."

—*Ephesians 2:10 (NIV)*

MiracleofMax.com

Scan the QR code to learn more about how you can use The Miracle of Max to raise funds for your nonprofit. Or contact miracleofmax@gmail.com.

Follow Max on social media:

Author Biographies

Stephanie and Stephen McChesney are not just parents but advocates, entrepreneurs, and a testament to the power of faith and love. Their journey began with the birth of their son, Max, a miracle child who redefined their perspective on life. Together, they have navigated the world of special needs, participating in and championing causes such as the Tim Tebow Foundation's Night to Shine and spearheading the Best Buddies International chapter in South Carolina. Their involvement in these initiatives reflects their dedication to making the world a more inclusive and loving place.

In the professional realm, Stephanie and Stephen are the dynamic duo behind the successful Skin by Stephanie practices, located in both Charleston and the Greenville area. Their entrepreneurial spirit doesn't stop there; they are also the creators of Science Ceuticals, a line of high-performance cosmeceutical products that marry science with skincare.

Proud parents to Max and Madeline, Stephanie and Stephen's lives are a blend of personal and professional triumphs. Their love for their children is paralleled only by their affection for their fur babies, Coco Chanel and Sebastian.

At the heart of their story is a deep and abiding love for family, friends, and Jesus Christ. Their journey, marked by challenges, triumphs, and unwavering faith, serves as an inspiration to many. Through their book, *The Miracle of Max,* they hope to share a message of resilience, hope, and the endless possibilities that come with believing in the miraculous.

Made in the USA
Columbia, SC
20 January 2024